CW00656362

KNOOPS

Chocolate recipes through the day

ISBN 978-1-5272-9409-7
knoops.co.uk

Contents

About Knoops

My obsession with chocolate stems from my childhood in Germany. Whenever I had been good, or done something well, my grandmother would reward me with a piece of chocolate. She was quite ceremonial about it, making sure I sat on a chair and waited for the moment. It was so special and magical, and it was then that I fell in love with chocolate. It has always held happy and positive associations for me.

With a passion for both chocolate and cooking, my own experimental approach to flavour also stems from my early childhood. When I was growing up in Germany in the 1970's, there was hardly any international cuisine available, yet my mother was inspired to discover Spanish, Italian and Greek cooking. The dishes she prepared for us were exotic and exciting, broadening not only our palates but our horizons. She always wanted to try something different using new herbs and spices, and cooking using new and different techniques.

This experimentation with new flavours and methods was her way of welcoming the outside world into our home; it is reflected today in what I do with Knoopology, the art of creating the perfect chocolate drink. I like to offer everyone the opportunity to explore different taste combinations as unconventional as they dare, from cinnamon to Szechuan pepper, matcha and lemon zest to saffron. Each herb, spice and fruit we add unleashes a different combination to enhance the underlying chocolate flavour. Adding savoury and herbal flavours to the sweetness of white or milk chocolate creates a pleasing balance, and the intense flavours of our dark chocolates can be enhanced with a touch of spice or citrus. That is what I want people to experience in store with my trained Knoopologists.

Chocolate continues to amaze me with its complexity and the range of experiences it evokes. Sweet or bitter, it is a pure escape to the country where the beans were grown; whether Madagascar, Colombia, Venezuela or the Solomon Islands, each has its own distinct flavour and underlying notes. Fine chocolate flavours change as you let them unfurl in your mouth. With Knoops, I wanted to create a way to inspire people to experiment and show them what is possible. In just two minutes, we can create the ideal chocolate drink for anyone, whether they choose a 28% white chocolate or a 72% dark Peruvian chocolate. We can use any kind of milk as a base, and add an array of spices and seasonings ranging from sea salt, or chilli, to orange zest, pink peppercorns or nutmeg. The flavour combinations are infinite, and each enhances and marries particularly well with a certain percentage and origin. The theatre of making the chocolate, and engaging with it, is so important and personal. For me it is as much about the chocolate as the service. Whether hot or cold, our chocolate drinks become fully interactive, conceived together, in the moment.

I left Germany to study fine art photography and ended up travelling extensively in the Caribbean as well as Japan, China, Thailand, Hong Kong and

7

Singapore. The amazing new flavours and taste combinations I experienced on my travels profoundly influenced me. I always knew I wanted to make my career doing something that brings happiness, and to incorporate my passion for chocolate with the incredible flavours I discovered on my travels; so, the first Knoops café was born in the old town of Rye in 2013. The desire for small, attainable, everyday luxuries makes perfect sense to me, and I felt that there was a gap in the market when it came to providing people with real drinking chocolate.

Knoops focuses on a carefully curated collection of chocolate percentages and origins, which can be enjoyed pure or enhanced with added natural flavours; this is the process I call Knoopology. The Knoops concept is based around our specialist percentage menu, which offers a wide range of chocolates to suit all tastes. The menu options run from a balanced and creamy 28% white chocolate to a rich and naturally sugar-free 100% extra dark. Between the two sits an exciting array of ruby, milk, and dark chocolates from some of the world's best chocolate-growing regions in Central and South America, Asia, Africa and Oceania.

With Knoops I can create a special something for everyone, and now you can recreate the experience at home. Our range of different chocolate percentages, flaked by Knoops in Sussex, provides plenty of choice for drinking, cooking, baking and garnishing, depending on your palate. The recipes in this book provide ample opportunity to experiment.

To make the drinks you can use any of our hand-picked hot chocolate makers to recreate that unique Knoops experience with the traditional froth. Float one of our famously delicious marshmallows on top for 'a hug in a mug'. White porcelain bowls are the very best way to serve Knoops hot chocolate drinks; cradle one in your hands to enjoy the warmth as you sip your way through the foam to the goodness that lies beneath.

This book contains my favourite 40 drinks and 20 dishes from around the world, created using a range of the Knoops chocolate percentages. The intention is that these can be enjoyed — as moments of respite and pleasure, in company or alone — throughout the day. Beginning with breakfast, the recipes move on to elevenses then lunch, tea-time then supper, followed by after-dinner snacks and cocktails, and the book closes with my favourite night-caps, to prepare you for restorative sleep. Both savoury and sweet dishes are included, some are very chocolatey and indulgent, and others (such as the Chilli con carne and the Chicory salad), are enhanced with the addition of chocolate to add earthy and rich undertones. You will discover in these pages an array of incredible drinks; both hot and cold. Some are nutritious, some pure pleasure, and others refreshing and comforting. There are excellent cocktails to share with friends, and exciting dinner and pudding suggestions for entertaining family and friends alike.

There is a glorious alchemy at work when pouring heated milk onto chocolate, releasing and expanding all the glorious and diverse flavours. I would say the process sits somewhere between art and science.

Jens

A Little About Chocolate

Chocolate has been consumed as a drink for most of its long history. At Knoops, we are proud to continue this ancient tradition with our own drinking chocolate. We use only the finest chocolate flakes, the most versatile way to enjoy this incredible ingredient.

The cacao plant, its pods containing the precious beans from which chocolate is made, originates in the Upper Amazon. The geographical area in which cacao can grow is limited to within 20 degrees north and south of the equatorial belt, due to climate and soil, but most is grown within just 10 degrees of the equator. The earliest evidence of cacao use by humans was found in southeastern Ecuador, dated to several thousand years ago, and we know from archaeological records that cacao was highly valued as a drink in pre-Colombian cultures of Mesoamerica, such as the Olmec. For several centuries, the beans were even used as currency.

Early peoples, including the Maya and later the Aztecs, first treated cacao as a fruit, eating the white pulp around the bitter beans. Cacao pulp tastes glorious, like lychee spritzed with lime. It was used to make drinks, both fresh and fermented into alcohol. At some point, people experimented with treating cacao beans in much the same way they treated corn and other edible grains and seeds – by sun-drying, roasting and grinding them. But they would have discovered that these beans behaved rather differently. A cacao bean is 40-60% fat (cocoa butter), and when the beans are ground this fat is released and forms a paste, 'chocolate'. Early on, this chocolate was combined with other ingredients — spices like vanilla or chilli, herbs, flowers, honey and grains — and consumed in different kinds of drinks. A thin, corn-based porridge was popular. Frothy drinks, with thick foam on top, were particularly prized, even considered sacred. The foam, created by pouring chocolate repeatedly from one bowl to another to aerate it, was regarded as a significant gift, a drink that honoured the recipient. These frothy chocolate drinks were enjoyed by royals and nobles, and often consumed on special occasions. We honour this grand tradition by topping all Knoops drinks with enticing froth. We have made it easy for you to recreate this froth at home too, using our special chocolate shakers.

In the early 1500s, cacao beans from Latin America arrived in Spain and chocolate became popular with the Spanish aristocracy. They added sugar, spices, and heated the drink. Spain established cacao plantations in its overseas colonies, to feed the growing demand. During the same century, the Spanish Inquisition saw Jews fleeing persecution and travelling across Europe. Some carried cacao with them, as well as the tools and expertise required to make it delicious.

In Jamaica, the eminent 18th-century physician Hans Sloane was introduced to cacao as a drink favoured by the local people. He found it 'nauseous' but discovered that mixing it with milk made it more palatable. He brought cacao back to England where, mixed with milk and fortified with egg, he fed it to undernourished poor children in London.

In the early 1800s, Conrad Van Houten from The Netherlands discovered a way to press cocoa butter out of ground cacao beans. The dry 'cake' left behind when the cocoa butter was removed was ground into cocoa powder. This was easier than the beans to work with, and chocolate drinking became universally accessible.

It wasn't until the late 1800s that recipes appeared featuring chocolate in anything other than drinks. By this point almost all drinking chocolate was made with the now widely-available cocoa powder. Hans

Sloane's recipe was initially sold by apothecaries as medication, but was adopted by Cadbury later in the 19th century, and adapted with cocoa powder. The invention of cocoa powder also sparked the creation of a rudimentary eating chocolate.

J. S. Fry & Sons produced the first solid chocolate bar in 1847, and Cadbury created its first in 1849. In Switzerland in 1879, Rodolphe Lindt then developed a way to process the whole beans to a smooth paste, also known as conching.

Introduction

Chocolate the Superfood

Real chocolate is a true superfood, packed with vitamins and minerals to energise, heal, nourish and soothe. It provides wonderful health benefits, as well as a delicious taste experience that makes us feel great. Modern industrial confectionery bars contain only the very smallest amount of actual chocolate.

Stick with the best. We have chocolates for everyone, regardless of preference or palate, to suit any occasion, mood, or time of day. We have chocolate to uplift and energise, to calm and quiet, to replenish and restore. Cacao beans contain theobromine and caffeine, which act as stimulants, and these are more concentrated in higher percentage chocolates. Therefore, dark chocolate is the best choice for a pick-me-up. Milk chocolate — with added protein and sugar — is a reminder for many of us of our childhoods, a gentle nostalgia-nudge. White chocolate, made with only cocoa butter, milk and sugar, is pure comfort.

At Knoops, we present a variety of vegan and dairy chocolates, plant-based and dairy milks, and additional flavours. We offer you a bespoke chocolate experience; whether you are looking for a brain boost, an energy lift, a post-workout refuel, something special to share or a home-time treat... you've come to the right place.

Ingredients

Chocolate

All chocolates featured in this book are from our own Knoops range. Each has been carefully chosen for its quality and flavour profile.

Generally, when choosing chocolate for a recipe, try to use the percentage and origin specified where possible. The recipe will have been developed with that sweetness and flavour profile in mind and may not work so well if you deviate too far from it. For example, a recipe that specifies a 100% chocolate may not benefit from the sugar if you use a 65% instead. Of course, once you are confident with a recipe one of the joys of cooking with chocolate is playing with flavour combinations and using your favourites. But bear in mind sweetness and strength levels in particular when experimenting.

A note about percentage

The percentage of a chocolate is a rough indicator of its sweetness. It denotes the quantity of cocoa solids in the recipe, which means anything that derives from the cocoa bean, including cocoa mass (the whole ground bean) and cocoa butter (the fat from the bean). This is why white chocolate can have a cocoa percentage, although it only contains cocoa butter. It is the knowledgeable selection of cocoa beans and the expertise of the chocolate maker that is an indicator of quality. Percentage alone is not. There may be vastly different flavour notes within chocolates of the same percentage depending on various factors. So, for example, not all 70% chocolates will have the same flavour or intensity; they will vary in flavour depending on the different beans and their regions of origin. Moreover, the residual 30% can be made up of various other ingredients, such as vanilla, sugar, or emulsifiers.

Dark chocolate

Dark chocolate is made from cocoa beans (cocoa mass/cocoa solids) and sugar (except 100% which has no sugar), with the possible addition of natural vanilla and soy lecithin (a natural product used to aid emulsification).

Milk chocolate

Milk chocolate contains cocoa beans (cocoa mass/cocoa solids), powdered milk and sugar, with the possible addition of natural vanilla and soy lecithin.

White chocolate

White chocolate contains cocoa butter (the fatty part of the cocoa bean), powdered milk and sugar, with the possible addition of natural vanilla and soy lecithin.

Measuring chocolate

When using a teaspoon to measure out your chocolate flakes, one teaspoon weighs between four and five grams, depending on the size of the flakes.

Melting chocolate

Care must be taken when melting chocolate. If it comes into contact with water, the chocolate will seize. If the chocolate overheats, it will burn. If either of these things happen you will need to start from scratch. The easiest way to melt chocolate is in a bain marie (a bowl resting over a pan of hot water). You must ensure that the water is kept clear of the chocolate, and that the bottom of the bowl is well above the water. If you do not use all the chocolate at once, it can be reheated and melted again as necessary. If using direct heat in a pan, or using a microwave, choose the lowest heat settings, be cautious, and keep a close eye on the chocolate. Once most of the chocolate is melted, you can stop heating. Any remaining lumps will melt in the residual heat, encouraged by gentle stirring with a spatula.

Storing chocolate

Chocolate absorbs other flavours easily, so it is best to store it away from strong smelling foods. This, combined with the fact that chocolate doesn't keep well in a moist environment, means that it is not a good idea to store chocolate in the fridge. Chocolate keeps best stored in an airtight container in a cool, dry environment, somewhere between 18°C and 20°C.

Alternative Ingredients

Milk and alternative milks

Unless otherwise specified, the recipes in this book use full fat cows' milk throughout. If a recipe works better with a different milk, it will be noted. Do try all the recipes with your favourite milks, just note that all milks behave differently, and will create varying amounts of froth. Instore at Knoops, all our drinks are available with a range of cows' milk and plant-based milks.

Gluten free

Unless otherwise stated, all recipes use ordinary flour, but these can usually be substituted with an appropriate gluten-free flour. Please bear in mind that this might require greater attention when baking in terms of a lower baking temperature, and/or a little additional liquid, an extra egg or additional ½ tsp of baking powder.

Equipment

For the most authentic Knoops experience, all the chocolate drinks in this book have been made with our chocolate shaker or one of our milk frothers, both available in-store and through our website. Hob and microwave are of course alternative options for heating the milk.

Breakfast

Do you want breakfast on the go, with all the nutrition in one drink?
Try our Breakfast shake and Fruit smoothie. Both include some chocolate
for extra deliciousness.

Breakfast shake

A vegan breakfast boost.

Serves

Ingredients

1 banana

4 tsp oatmeal

1 tsp milled chia seeds

1 tsp honey

6 tsp (approx. 25g) 65%
dark chocolate flakes

1 scant tsp smooth peanut
butter

1 tsp lemon juice

150ml oat milk

Method

Blend all ingredients together
until smooth.

Pour into a large glass and serve.

Fruit smoothie

A berry-loaded vegan smoothie
full of energy and vitamins.

Serves

Ingredients

1 banana

50g blueberries

50g raspberries

50g strawberries

½ tsp fresh ginger, freshly
grated

150ml oat milk

1 tsp honey

6 tsp (approx. 25g) 54%
dark chocolate flakes

20g walnuts

Method

Blend all ingredients, except the walnuts
and 1 tsp of the chocolate, until very
smooth. Add the nuts and the remaining
chocolate flakes and blend again briefly,
to retain some great texture.

Pour into a large glass and serve.

Baked churros

A take on the delicious Spanish breakfast snack, but a little healthier as these are baked rather than deep fried. Enjoy them fresh from the oven, with a bowl of luxurious melted dipping chocolate.

Ingredients

60g unsalted butter

1 tbsp unrefined caster sugar

½ tsp vanilla paste

125ml water

75g plain white flour, sifted

A small pinch of salt

2 eggs

Icing sugar for dusting

For dipping

150g 54% dark chocolate

Method

Preheat the oven to 200°C (180°C fan), Gas 6, 400°F.

Place butter, sugar, vanilla paste, water and salt in a medium saucepan and bring to a simmer. Remove the pan from the heat and add the sifted flour. Use a flat spatula to combine thoroughly.

Return the saucepan to a gentle heat for one minute, stirring continuously with the spatula to cook the flour without it sticking or changing colour. Remove from heat and transfer mixture to a large bowl.

Whisk both eggs together in a small bowl. Add a quarter of the whisked egg to the flour mixture and stir thoroughly with the spatula until fully combined. Repeat this process to slowly incorporate the rest of the eggs until you have a well-combined batter that falls off the spatula. You may not need to use all of the eggs to reach this consistency, which is why adding them slowly is essential. If the batter is too runny, the churros will not hold their shape.

Spoon the batter into a piping bag fitted with a 15mm star nozzle. Carefully pipe the dough into 10cm lengths, making sure they are not too thin. Leave spaces between each piece to allow the churros enough room to expand as they bake.

Bake for 20-30 minutes until golden and puffy. Then remove the churros from the oven and quickly pierce each with a skewer to release any steam. Place them on a cooling rack to dry.

Gently melt the chocolate in a small bowl over a saucepan of simmering water, then pour into a dipping bowl. Dust the churros with icing sugar, then serve alongside the melted dipping chocolate – divine!

Chocolate and tea make a beautiful pairing; the fragrance of the tea elevates the smooth sweetness or robust intensity of each carefully-chosen chocolate. These recipes include other aromatics as well, to lift and round out the flavours.

Hot chocolate, Earl Grey & lemon zest

Serves

1

Ingredients

200ml milk

½ tsp lemon zest

1 Earl Grey teabag

8 tsp (approx. 34g) 70% chocolate flakes

Method

Heat milk with the lemon zest. When milk is steaming, add the teabag and infuse for one minute. Remove the teabag. Add the chocolate flakes and whisk until well blended (or combine in a chocolate shaker).

Pour and serve.

Hot chocolate, Lapsang Souchong & orange zest

Serves

1

Ingredients

200ml milk

1 tsp orange zest

I lapsang souchong teabag

8 tsp (approx. 34g) 54% chocolate flakes

Method

Heat milk with the orange zest. When the milk is steaming, add the teabag and infuse for one minute. Remove the teabag. Add chocolate flakes and whisk until well blended (or combine in a chocolate shaker).

Pour and serve.

Masala chocolate chai

Laced with luxurious flavours inspired by sweet Indian spiced tea, this warming and distinctive blend is also delicious served cold.

Ingredients

6 green cardamom pods

1 star anise

5 black peppercorns

½ cinnamon stick

2 cloves

1 thin slice of fresh ginger

1 tsp loose-leaf Darjeeling tea (or 1 tea bag)

8 tsp (approx. 34g) 34% milk chocolate flakes

Method

Crush the spices in a pestle and mortar to break them up a little. Heat the milk with the tea and spices until warm, and then leave to infuse for five minutes. Heat the milk to steaming point, then strain over the chocolate flakes. Whisk to melt and blend, or combine in a chocolate shaker.

Pour and serve.

Bicerin

This drink is inspired by the traditional Italian mocha; the original has been served at its birthplace, the Caffè Al Bicerin in Turin, since 1763.

Ingredients

100ml single cream

150ml milk

20 tsp (approx. 85g) 72% chocolate flakes

4 shots of espresso coffee

Method

Whisk the cream well to aerate it.

Heat milk to steaming point. Whisk chocolate flakes into the milk until melted and fully incorporated, or combine in a chocolate shaker.

Make the espresso, and pour into four glasses. Divide the hot chocolate between them, pouring carefully over the coffee.

Spoon the cream into the top of each, and serve.

Ⓚ Knoops Tip: 100ml frothed milk can be spooned on top as an alternative to the cream if preferred. Sprinkle with dark chocolate flakes to finish.

Chocolate granola

A delicious, nutritious, energy-packed way to start your day.

Ingredients

100g almonds

40g hazelnuts

40g cashew nuts

60g sunflower seeds

60g pumpkin seeds

300g whole oats

1 tsp cinnamon

1 tsp nutmeg

1 tsp ground cardamom

¼ tsp salt

6 tbsp maple syrup

6 tbsp honey

3 tbsp water

2 tbsp vegetable oil (such as groundnut oil)

2 tbsp butter

6 tbsp (70g) 70% dark chocolate flakes

To finish

An extra large handful of 70% dark chocolate flakes

Method

Preheat the oven to 150°C (130°C fan), Gas 2, 300°F. Line a large baking tray with baking paper.

Roughly chop all the nuts and place in a large bowl with the seeds and oats. Stir in spices and salt.

Warm the maple syrup, honey, water, oil and butter in a small saucepan until well combined. Pour the syrup mix over the nuts, seeds and oat mix, and stir well to combine.

Spread the mixture evenly over the prepared baking tray. Bake the granola for approximately 15–20 minutes, checking it at regular intervals, and turning with a spoon or spatula each time to prevent sticking or burning. While the granola is baking, melt the chocolate in a bowl over a pan of simmering water.

Once the granola is an even golden-brown colour, remove the tray from the oven. Pour over the melted chocolate, combining everything using a spatula, then return to the oven for five more minutes.

Remove granola from the oven, and allow to cool completely.

Stir through the extra handful of chocolate flakes to enhance the flavour and crunch. Store in an airtight container; the granola will keep for up to two weeks.

🄚 **Knoops Tip:** This granola pairs perfectly with yogurt and berries.

Champurrado

A water-based breakfast hot chocolate, thickened with cornflour and lightly spiced, *champurrado* is the chocolate version of *atole* — the traditional cornmeal-based Mexican drink. Whilst we have suggested the addition of cayenne pepper, *champurrado* can be flavoured with a number of different spices. Experiment to find your favourite flavours.

Ingredients

½ cinnamon stick

500ml water

85g 65% dark chocolate flakes

3 tbsp Harina de Maiz blanco (pre-cooked white maize meal) mixed with 8 tbsp of cold water

⅛ tsp cayenne pepper

Method

Place the cinnamon stick in the water and heat to a low simmer. Then add the chocolate flakes, whisking to melt and incorporate.

When smooth, add the Harina de Maiz and heat gently, whisking as the mixture thickens. Whisk in the cayenne pepper to season.

Remove the cinnamon stick, or strain if necessary. Pour into mugs or bowls, sprinkle with cayenne pepper, and serve immediately.

Dark chocolate, pecan & prune muffins

Dark chocolate and prunes make a wonderful combination for a classic breakfast muffin. Spelt and most gluten-free flours work very well in this recipe.

Ingredients

150g unsalted butter

2 large eggs

1 tsp vanilla extract

285ml buttermilk

150g plain flour

150g wholemeal flour

2 tsp baking powder

1 tsp bicarbonate of soda

Pinch of salt

185g unrefined caster sugar

100g roughly chopped pecans

100g 65% dark chocolate flakes

100g roughly chopped soft prunes

For the topping

60g chopped soft prunes

60g chopped pecans

1 tbsp demerara sugar

To finish

Icing sugar

Method

Preheat the oven to 190°C (170°C fan), Gas 5, 375°F.
Line a twelve-cup muffin tray with large paper muffin cases.

Melt the butter, then allow to cool a little. Pour into a large jug and whisk together with the eggs, vanilla and buttermilk until well combined.

Place the flours, baking powder, bicarbonate of soda, salt and sugar into a large mixing bowl, and stir to combine. Make a well in the centre of these dry ingredients.

Pour the buttermilk mixture into the well and stir through with a large spatula until all ingredients are only just combined. It is important not to overmix if you want light fluffy muffins. The mixture will remain lumpy looking, just check you don't have any pockets of unincorporated flour. Add the pecans, chocolate and prunes, folding them in with just a couple of strokes.

Spoon the muffin mixture into your paper cases, dividing evenly. Mix the topping ingredients together in a small bowl, then spoon equal amounts on top of each muffin.

Bake the muffins for 20 minutes, until they are well risen and the topping is crisp. Cool in the tin for about five minutes, then remove from the tin and finish cooling on a wire rack.

Lightly dust with icing sugar before serving.

Santafereño

This popular Colombian breakfast drink consists of gently spiced hot chocolate poured over cheese. Enjoy with a spoon to scoop out the delicious melting cheese, with a good hunk of bread alongside. Who would have thought chocolate and cheese could taste so delicious together?

Ingredients

200ml milk

1 stick of cinnamon

Grated nutmeg

3 or 4 cubes of edam cheese

8 tsp (approx. 34g) 65% chocolate flakes

Method

Heat the milk with the spices and allow to infuse for five minutes. Place the cheese cubes in your mug or drinking bowl. Reheat milk until steaming, then add the chocolate flakes and whisk until well blended, or combine in a chocolate shaker.

Pour the piping hot chocolate milk over the cheese, and serve with a spoon.

Easy iced mocha

This is a simple, refreshing take on the classic coffee and chocolate flavour combination.

Ingredients

4 tsp (approx. 16g) 54% dark chocolate flakes (or chocolate of your choice)

1 shot of double espresso

Cold milk or water

3 ice cubes

Method

This drink is best made in a chocolate shaker. Add chocolate to the shaker, then pour over the hot coffee. Shake until the chocolate has melted. Top up the shaker with your preferred amount of milk, or use cold water. Add the ice cubes, then shake again.

Pour into a glass and serve.

Elevenses

Knoops mocha

This mocha was born in our Knoops store in Rye, and proved a popular pick-me-up from the very first day. It is warming, uplifting and comforting all in one delicious drink.

It is dedicated to Graham Wickens, without whom there would be no Knoops.

Ingredients

200ml milk

½ tsp cinnamon

¼ tsp nutmeg

Small pinch of chilli powder

8 tsp (approx. 34g) 54% chocolate flakes

A double shot of espresso

Method

Heat the milk with the spices. When the milk is steaming, whisk in the chocolate flakes until well blended (or combine in a chocolate shaker).

Pour the espresso over the spiced hot chocolate and serve.

Energy bars

A power-packed combination of nuts, seeds, fruit and flavour, dipped in dark chocolate to give that extra energy boost.

Ingredients

100g flaked almonds

50g pumpkin seeds

75g sunflower seeds

25g sesame seeds

150g unsalted butter

300g unrefined caster sugar

3 tbsp (60g) golden syrup

2 tbsp (40g) maple syrup

350g jumbo oats

½ tsp ground ginger

A large pinch of salt

100g dried cranberries

150g 65% dark chocolate flakes

Method

Preheat oven to 200°C (180°C fan), Gas 6, 400°F.
Prepare two nine-cavity financier moulds, preferably silicone.

Heat the almonds and seeds in a dry frying pan over a low heat, until they start to colour and you can smell them toasting. Then set aside to cool.

Melt butter, sugar and syrups together in a saucepan large enough to hold all the ingredients, until just bubbling. Remove pan from the heat and stir in the oats, ground ginger and salt, and then the almonds, seeds and dried fruit. Stir thoroughly until all ingredients are well coated. Press the mixture down into the financier moulds, and level so the surfaces are flat and even. Leave ½-cm space at the top, to allow room for the chocolate layer (added after baking).

Place filled moulds into the oven and bake for approximately 20-25 minutes until golden on top and bubbling at the edges. The bars will then be sufficiently caramelised to hold together. Remove from the oven and leave in the moulds to cool on a wire rack.

While cooling, melt chocolate flakes in a bowl over a pan of simmering water, then spread the chocolate evenly over the top of each bar to fill the ½-cm spaces. Chill in the fridge or freezer to set the chocolate layer. Once chocolate is completely set, turn out your bars. Store in an airtight container.

Bircher muesli smoothie

Packed with protein, this smoothie is great post-workout and excellent for muscle recovery. Satisfying, nutritious, and delicious any time of day, it includes nuts, yogurt, fresh apples and overnight-soaked oats.

Ingredients

100g porridge oats

300g apple juice

50g walnuts

2 Granny Smith apples

400g full fat Greek yogurt

60g 72% dark chocolate flakes

Method

Place porridge oats in a bowl and pour over the apple juice. Cover and soak until soft (overnight).

Chop or grind the walnuts in a food processor until finely ground. Add peeled and roughly chopped apples, yogurt, and chocolate. Add overnight oats and apple juice. Process until fully combined and a drinkable consistency. Add more apple juice for a thinner consistency if desired.

Pour into tall glasses and serve.

Rocky road

No baking here, just some melting, mixing, and cooling, followed by a delicious treat. This can be made using any gluten-free biscuits if you prefer.

Ingredients

200g unsalted butter

600g 54% dark chocolate flakes

300g golden syrup

300g Rich Tea or digestive biscuits, or any other favourite biscuits

200g dried cranberries

200g Knoops marshmallows, cut into 5-cm pieces

Method

Line a 20 x 30 cm brownie tin with baking paper, leaving some hanging over the sides so you can easily lift the rocky road from the tin later.

In a pan, melt butter, chocolate and syrup together over a medium heat, stirring to mix well. Remove from heat and set aside to cool a little.

Break the biscuits into pieces and place them into a large bowl with the cranberries and marshmallow pieces. Pour over the chocolate mixture and stir quickly to coat everything. Use as few strokes as possible, so the marshmallows don't melt.

Pour the mixture into the prepared brownie pan, smoothing down so the top is even. Place the rocky road in the fridge for a few hours, or overnight, to cool and harden.

Remove from the tin. Cut into 32 evenly-sized pieces and store in an airtight container. This can also be frozen.

White chocolate matcha

Matcha perfectly balances the sweetness of white chocolate, and gives this drink its beautifully fresh green colour.

Ingredients

200ml whole milk

8 tsp (approx. 34g) 28% white chocolate flakes

1 tsp matcha powder

Method

Heat milk to steaming point. Whisk in the chocolate flakes and matcha until well blended (or combine in a chocolate shaker).

Pour and serve immediately.

Banana bread

This banana bread is completely delicious, just remember to use very ripe bananas. The dark chocolate and banana flavours complement each other perfectly, and this recipe works just as well with gluten-free flour. Thick slices are best.

Ingredients

100g unsalted butter

110g unrefined caster sugar

2 beaten eggs

220g plain flour or gluten-free flour

2 tsp baking powder

¼ tsp bicarbonate of soda

½t tsp ground ginger

½ tsp ground cinnamon

3 large very ripe bananas +
1 banana for decoration

50g chopped walnuts

75g dark chocolate flakes
(our 72% works well here)

2-3 tbsp milk

1 tbsp runny honey
for glazing

Method

Preheat oven to 180°C (160°C fan) Gas 4, 350°F.
Grease or line a loaf tin.

Beat the butter and sugar together in a large bowl until creamy, then add the beaten egg. Stir together the flour, baking powder, bicarbonate of soda, and spices in a separate bowl.

Mash the bananas in another bowl and add to the butter, sugar and egg mix. Gradually add the dry ingredients, continuously beating until everything is incorporated.

Finally, stir through the nuts and chocolate so they are evenly distributed. Gradually add the milk, tablespoon by tablespoon, and mix briefly to create a smooth batter (you may not need to use all the milk).

Pour into the prepared loaf tin. Slice the last banana in half lengthways and place on each side of the top of the loaf. Glaze with honey and scatter a few chopped walnuts over to finish.

Bake in the centre of the oven for 50 minutes, checking after 40, and again at five-minute intervals until a skewer inserted into the centre comes out clean.

Turn out onto a wire rack to cool. Cut into thick slices, and serve.

Chocolate float

This is our take on the American diner classic, using chocolate milk instead of a soda. This could be made vegan with non-dairy milk and ice cream and, of course, delicious dark chocolate.

Serves

Ingredients

6 tsp (approx. 25g) your favourite chocolate flakes

220ml milk

2 scoops of vanilla ice cream

Method

Add chocolate flakes to 70 ml of milk in a shaker. Heat in the microwave for a few seconds, just long enough to start melting the chocolate. Shake to combine the milk and the chocolate.

Add the rest of the milk and one scoop of ice cream and shake again.

Pour into a tall, chilled glass, top with the second scoop of ice cream, and serve immediately.

Iced chocolate milk

A classic chocolate drink with either dairy or non-dairy milk, best made in a shaker. Popular with the whole family, and a great replenisher after a workout.

Serves

Ingredients

6 tsp (approx. 25g) your favourite chocolate flakes

220ml milk

3 ice cubes

Method

Add chocolate flakes to 70 ml of milk in a shaker. Heat in the microwave for a few seconds, just long enough to start melting the chocolate. Shake to combine the milk and the chocolate.

Add the rest of the milk, along with the ice cubes, and shake again.

Pour into a tall, chilled glass and serve immediately.

Lunch

Chocolate & raspberry lassi

The depth of dark chocolate and the tartness of raspberry is a perfect pairing. A novel take on the classic Indian yogurt drink.

Ingredients

10 tsp (approx. 42g) 54% dark chocolate flakes

15g sugar

250ml full fat yogurt

300ml cold milk

35g raspberries + 6-8 extra to decorate

Method

Melt the chocolate and sugar in 50ml of the milk, heating just enough to melt the chocolate. Whisk until smooth. Pour into a large jug with all the other ingredients and blend with a stick blender until smooth and well mixed.

Pour into tall glasses, decorate with extra raspberries and a sprinkle of chocolate flakes, and serve.

Chicory, pear, blue cheese & walnut salad

The contrasting and complementary flavours of this crisp autumnal salad are as delicious as the colours on the plate.

Ingredients

Dressing

5g 100% dark chocolate flakes

1 tbsp sherry vinegar

1 tbsp mirin

4 tbsp olive oil

Salt

Ground pepper

Salad

2 ripe pears

2 heads red chicory

120g full-flavoured blue cheese such as Gorgonzola, Roquefort or Stilton

12 walnut halves, roughly chopped

A couple of pinches 100% dark chocolate flakes

Method

Whisk together the dark chocolate, vinegar and mirin. Microwave for 10 seconds, or heat in a small pan over a low heat, then whisk again to melt the chocolate. Once the chocolate is combined well with the vinegar and mirin, add olive oil and whisk briskly to blend. Season with salt and pepper to taste.

Slice the pears and arrange on plates. Separate the chicory leaves and scatter them on top, followed by the chopped walnuts. Pour the dressing lightly over everything. Break the cheese into bite-sized pieces and dot across the plates.

Finally, sprinkle chocolate flakes lightly over each plate, and serve.

Chocolate milkshake

Have you ever met a child who didn't love a milkshake? This delicious chocolate version is the perfect treat, whatever your age. Whether you shake or blend, this should be enjoyed immediately.

Ingredients

150ml cold milk

8 tsp (approx. 34g) 34% milk chocolate flakes for a sweet drink, or use 70% chocolate flakes for something a little darker

2 scoops vanilla ice cream

Classic method

Warm 50ml of the milk and the chocolate for a few seconds in the microwave, then blend to combine. Top up with the rest of the milk, add the ice cream and blend until smooth.

Pour into a tall glass and serve.

Shaker method

Put the chocolate and 50ml of the milk in the shaker, microwave for a few seconds, then shake to melt and blend. Top up with the rest of the milk. Add the ice cream in small spoonfuls. Shake again, pour into a tall glass, and serve.

ⓚ **Knoops Tip:** Whip 50ml cream and pipe on top to decorate, finishing with a sprinkle of chocolate flakes.

Red pepper & puy lentil salad

This salad is wonderful to share, for a delicious lunch outdoors. The addition of 100% chocolate flakes adds an earthy depth of flavour to the lentils.

Ingredients

The Salad

4 red peppers

8-10 thyme sprigs

1 clove garlic, finely sliced

Olive oil to drizzle

Sea salt

Ground pepper

300g Puy or small brown lentils

1 vegetable or chicken stock cube

10g 100% dark chocolate flakes

50g rocket leaves

The Dressing

50ml olive oil

½ tsp cayenne pepper

2 tsp ground cumin

1 tbsp tomato puree

Juice of one lime

To Finish

50g flaked almonds

5g 100% dark chocolate flakes

Method

Preheat the oven to 190°C (170°C fan), Gas 5, 375°F.

Core and deseed the peppers. Arrange in a single layer in a roasting pan. Tuck in the thyme sprigs and scatter over the garlic. Drizzle peppers with oil and season with salt and pepper. Roast for 30-40 minutes until peppers are evenly cooked and caramelised at the edges. Remove from the oven, allow them to cool, then slip off their skins. Slice into thin rings.

While the peppers are roasting, rinse lentils in cold water and place them in a medium saucepan with just enough fresh water to cover. Simmer with the stock cube for 20 minutes, until the lentils are tender but still holding their shape. Remove lentils from heat and drain, then drizzle with olive oil. Season with salt and pepper.

Whisk all dressing ingredients together until smooth.

Spoon the lentils evenly into a shallow serving bowl or platter, sprinkle over chocolate flakes, cover with the rocket leaves and arrange the pepper slices on top. Drizzle with the dressing, and finish by sprinkling the flaked almonds and the remaining chocolate flakes over the top.

Serve at room temperature.

White chocolate pavlova

A pink and white chocolate twist on the classic meringue dessert. The meringue itself can be made a day or so ahead of time and kept in an airtight container or tin.

Ingredients

Meringue

6 egg whites (room temperature)

300g unrefined caster sugar

2 tsp cornflour, sifted

1 tsp white wine vinegar

1 tsp cream of tartar

100g 28% white or 47% ruby chocolate flakes

To serve

300ml whipping cream

200g raspberries

200g blackberries

50g ruby chocolate flakes

25g shelled pistachios, roughly chopped

Dark chocolate flakes

Method

Preheat your oven to 150°C (130°C fan) Gas 2, 300°F.
Begin by selecting a large mixing bowl. Ensure it is spotlessly clean and dry.

Whisk the egg whites in the bowl until they reach the soft peak stage. Add the sugar slowly, either spoonful by spoonful or in a thin steady stream, while whisking. Continue until all the sugar is incorporated and the mixture is thick and glossy without any grittiness. Gently fold through the sifted cornflour, the vinegar and the cream of tartar, folding for no longer than 30 seconds.

Spread the meringue into a 20cm circle on a lined baking tray. Gently raise the sides to form peaks, making sure the centre crater is shallower.

Place in the centre of the oven, then immediately lower the temperature to 120°C (100°C fan), Gas ½, 250°F for 75 minutes. Switch the oven off completely and leave the meringue inside, without opening the door, for a further 4-5 hours or overnight to cool completely.

Melt the 100g white or ruby chocolate flakes in a bowl over a saucepan of simmering water. Spread a thin layer over the meringue crater. Leave to set and form a crispy shell.

Just before serving, whip the cream to soft peaks and spoon into the meringue. Melt 50g ruby chocolate flakes in a bowl over a saucepan of simmering water, and use a spoon to drizzle over the whipped cream.

Cover with raspberries and blackberries, and sprinkle over the chopped pistachios.

Knoops Tip: Add quartered and sliced strawberries as well as, or instead of, the raspberries and blackberries, and any other berries as desired. Sprinkle over with dark chocolate flakes.

Chocolate affogato

A twist on the Italian classic. The ice cream here is drowned in both coffee and chocolate to make the perfect after-dinner treat. This affogato is dedicated to William for making my dreams come true.

Ingredients

1 single espresso

6 tsp (approx. 25g) 72% dark chocolate flakes

1 scoop vanilla ice cream

Method

Pour freshly-made espresso over the chocolate flakes in a jug and whisk to melt the chocolate. Place the ice cream in a glass serving dish.

Pour the mocha over the ice cream and serve.

Dark chocolate & marmalade bread & butter pudding

This decadent version of a traditional family pudding adds a zesty twist with the classic flavour combination of dark chocolate and orange.

Ingredients

100g unsalted butter, at room temperature

10-12 slices of brioche, crusts removed

200g orange marmalade

100g 65% dark chocolate flakes

800ml full fat milk

4 eggs

50g unrefined caster sugar

2 tbsp demerara sugar

Method

Butter each slice of brioche, using all the butter. Dot the marmalade over all slices, dividing evenly. Layer into a rectangular baking dish, sprinkling generously with chocolate as you tuck each slice into place. If you have any chocolate left at the end, sprinkle it over the top.

Whisk together milk, eggs and caster sugar in a jug, then pour evenly over the brioche slices. Sprinkle with the remaining demerara sugar for crunch, then set aside for half an hour.

Preheat oven to 180°C (160°C fan), Gas 4, 350°F.

After 30 minutes, place the pudding into the centre of the oven and bake for 35-40 minutes. It will puff up, turning golden and crisped at the edges.

Serve hot, dusted with icing sugar, alongside a jug of cold pouring cream or scoops of vanilla ice cream.

Teatime

Hot milk chocolate with mint & cinnamon

Mint and chocolate make a perfect pairing. Here they are combined with warming cinnamon, or try with a note of zesty lemon if you prefer.

Ingredients

200ml whole milk

8 tsp (approx. 34g) 34% milk chocolate flakes

4 fresh mint leaves

¼ tsp cinnamon or ½ tsp lemon zest, depending on your preference

Method

Heat milk with other ingredients together in a pan, whisking to combine and to melt the chocolate. If using a chocolate shaker, pour hot milk over the other ingredients in the shaker, then shake to melt the chocolate and combine.

Strain before pouring into a mug or bowl, and serve.

Triple layer chocolate cake

The ultimate showstopper for any celebration or special day. This beautiful cake brings back fond memories of Sunday afternoons with my mother and grandmother, a freshly-baked cake in pride of place on the table for the whole family to share.

Ingredients

For the cakes

400g 70% dark chocolate flakes

400g unsalted butter, plus extra for greasing tins

300g golden syrup

8 eggs

100g unrefined caster sugar

400g plain flour, sifted

150g ground almonds

2 tsp bicarbonate of soda

Pinch of salt

6 tbsp milk

For the ganache

700g 54% milk chocolate flakes

600ml double cream

Note: This makes enough to fill, top and ice the sides of the cake. If you just want to fill and top the cake, make just two-thirds of this quantity.

Method

Preheat oven to 180°C (160°C fan), Gas 4, 350°F.
Grease three 20-cm round cake tins.

Melt chocolate, butter and syrup in a pan over a low heat, stirring to combine. Whisk eggs with sugar in a large bowl until pale and mousse-like. Then add the melted chocolate mixture to the eggs, whisking until everything is fully incorporated. Fold in the flour, almonds, bicarbonate of soda and salt. Finally fold in the milk to form a smooth batter.

Divide the cake batter between the three tins and bake in the centre of the oven for 25-30 minutes. The cake is done when a skewer comes out clean. Cool the cakes on a wire rack in their tins.

Now prepare the ganache. Place milk chocolate flakes in a heatproof bowl. Heat the cream until just steaming, do not allow to simmer. Pour the hot cream over the chocolate and with small brisk movements, starting in the centre of the bowl, stir to combine. When the ganache is smooth leave to cool for about 30 minutes, until firm enough to spread.

Once the cakes are cool and the ganache firm, place the first cake on your serving plate. Spread one large spoonful of ganache across the top, then stack another cake carefully on top. Repeat until you have all three cakes stacked up and covered in ganache. Then take the remaining ganache and spread it carefully over the sides and top of the stacked cakes.

Slice, and enjoy.

Hot dark chocolate, Seville orange & smoked paprika

Only the smallest amount of smoked paprika (known as 'pimenton') is needed to complement the sweet fragrance of the Seville orange. Sprinkle some extra zest on top and the aroma will transport you to the warmth of a Mediterranean orange grove.

Ingredients

200ml whole milk

8 tsp (approx. 34g) 54% dark chocolate flakes

½ tsp freshly grated Seville orange zest (or other orange if Seville are not in season)

Very small pinch of smoked paprika, or chilli if you prefer heat without the smoked flavour

Method

Heat milk, until steaming but not boiling. Whisk all ingredients together to combine and melt the chocolate. Alternatively, pour the hot milk over other ingredients in a chocolate shaker, and shake to melt the chocolate and combine.

Pour into a mug or bowl, top with a little extra orange zest, and serve.

Hot dark chocolate, rosemary & star anise

I've always been a big fan of rosemary paired with chocolate. Adding a little star anise and a pinch of sea salt gives this drink a truly unique taste, reminding me of the salty liquorice of my childhood.

Ingredients

200ml whole milk

8 tsp (approx. 34g) 70% dark chocolate flakes

Leaves from ¼ sprig of rosemary

Half a star anise

Small pinch of sea salt

Small pinch of grated lemon zest

Method

Heat the milk, until steaming but not boiling. Whisk all ingredients together to combine and melt the chocolate. Alternatively, pour the hot milk over other ingredients in a chocolate shaker, and shake to melt the chocolate and combine.

Strain, pour into a mug or bowl, sprinkle with sea salt and serve.

Holly's hot milk chocolate, thyme, pink pepper & sea salt

Created by Holly, an expert Knoopologist and our longest-serving team member in Rye.

Ingredients

200ml whole milk

8 tsp (approx. 34g) 34% milk chocolate flakes

¼ to ½ tsp pink peppercorns, broken up using a pestle and mortar

A few leaves of fresh thyme

Scant ¼ tsp sea salt

Method

Heat all the ingredients together in a pan, whisking to combine and to melt the chocolate. If using a shaker, pour hot milk over the other ingredients, then shake to melt the chocolate and combine.

Strain, pour into a mug or bowl, and serve.

Viennese hot chocolate

This delicious hot chocolate is enriched with egg yolk, and topped with indulgent whipped cream. Sipping this will transport you to a café overlooking the Prater, or an Austrian ski resort on an icy winter's day.

Ingredients

150ml whole milk

8 tsp (approx. 34g) 65% dark chocolate flakes

One egg yolk

To serve

50ml whipped cream

65% dark chocolate flakes to scatter

Method

In a pan, heat the milk to steaming point. Add chocolate flakes and whisk until the chocolate is melted and combined. Whisk the egg yolk in a small bowl or jug, then add a spoonful or two of the warm milk and whisk to combine. Pour into the pan with the milk and chocolate. Heat again, whisking constantly for a few minutes until thickened.

Pour into a mug or glass. Top with whipped cream if desired, scatter with dark chocolate flakes, and serve.

Tiger cake

This cake is so named because when sliced it reveals gorgeous dark and white stripes. It is striking, fun and easy to make.

Ingredients

250g unsalted butter

250g unrefined caster sugar

4 eggs

250g self-raising flour

Pinch of salt

100g white chocolate flakes

½ tsp vanilla paste

100g 54% dark chocolate flakes

6 tbsp milk

To serve

Icing sugar, sifted

Method

Preheat oven to 170°C (150°C fan), Gas 3, 325°F. Grease a 24/25cm bundt tin or fluted cake ring.

Cream butter and sugar until light and creamy. Add the eggs one by one with a little of the flour to prevent curdling. Fold in the remaining flour and the salt. Divide the cake mixture into two separate bowls.

Melt white chocolate flakes in a small bowl over a simmering pan of water. Add the vanilla and three tablespoons of the milk to one bowl of the cake batter, along with the melted white chocolate. Fold the mixture gently until all is combined and the mixture drops easily from a spoon. If the batter is still too stiff, add a little extra milk.

Melt dark chocolate flakes in a small bowl over a simmering pan of water. Take the second bowl of cake batter and add the melted dark chocolate with the remaining milk. Mix until everything is smoothly combined, adding sufficient milk to ensure the batter drops easily from a spoon.

Spoon several alternate layers of the vanilla and chocolate batters into the greased tin until they are all used up, and lightly smooth down the surface.

Place the tin in the centre of the preheated oven for approximately 35 minutes, until a skewer inserted comes out clean. Bake for longer if necessary, checking at five-minute intervals. Cool the cake in its tin for about ten minutes, then turn it out onto a wire rack to cool completely.

Dust with icing sugar, slice, and serve.

Financiers

Legend has it that these sophisticated little French cakes are so named because they are wonderfully rich, and resemble gold bars. They make a great alternative to the better-known madeleines or macarons.

Ingredients

170g unsalted butter

120g ground almonds (or any of your favourite nuts)

40g flour

4 egg whites

140g icing sugar, sifted

To finish

30g 70% dark chocolate

30g 47% ruby chocolate

50g pistachios, shelled and chopped

Method

Preheat the oven to 160°C (140°C fan), Gas 3, 320°F. Prepare a nine-cavity financier mould. Financiers are best made in silicone moulds, but if using a metal mould prepare by brushing the cavities with a little melted butter.

In a small saucepan, melt the butter and continue to cook on a low heat, watching carefully, until you have a beurre noisette (once butter has started to brown and foam slightly). Then remove from heat.

In a mixing jug, combine ground almonds and flour. Whisk egg whites with the icing sugar into soft peak meringue. Gently fold in the almonds and flour with a spatula, until well combined. Slowly incorporate the melted noisette butter and continue to fold with the spatula until all is thoroughly mixed.

Pour the batter into the moulds; each should be two-thirds full. Bake the financiers for 20-25 minutes, until the little cakes are golden and firm to touch. Cool on a wire rack.

Melt both chocolates in separate bowls over simmering water. Decorate the cooled cakes one by one, dipping half of each financier into the dark chocolate, then drizzling with ruby chocolate as shown. Top with chopped pistachios and set aside until the chocolate has hardened.

Store in an airtight container, for no longer than two days.

We at Knoops are always on a mission to combine new flavours with our chocolates. Sometimes our customers bring us great suggestions. We love exploring flavours and experimenting with food pairings and new food trends.

Hot white chocolate, saffron & nutmeg	Hot white chocolate, ginger & lemon zest	Hot white chocolate, tarragon & star anise
Serves 1	Serves 1	Serves 1
Ingredients	**Ingredients**	**Ingredients**
200ml whole milk	200ml whole milk	200ml whole milk
8 tsp (approx. 34g) 28% white chocolate flakes	8 tsp (approx. 34g) 28% white chocolate flakes	8 tsp (approx. 34g) 28% white chocolate flakes
¼ tsp grated nutmeg	¼ tsp lemon zest	Leaves from one sprig of tarragon
⅛ tsp saffron	¼ tsp grated fresh ginger	Half a star anise
Method	**Method**	**Method**
Heat the milk until steaming but not boiling, and whisk all the ingredients together to combine and to allow the chocolate to melt. Alternatively, make by pouring heated milk over other ingredients in a chocolate shaker, and shake to combine.	Heat the milk until steaming but not boiling, and whisk all the ingredients together to combine and to allow the chocolate to melt. Alternatively, make by pouring heated milk over other ingredients in a chocolate shaker, and shake to combine.	Heat the milk until steaming but not boiling, and whisk all the ingredients together to combine and to allow the chocolate to melt. Alternatively, make by pouring heated milk over other ingredients in a chocolate shaker, and shake to combine.
Pour into a mug or bowl and serve.	Pour into a mug or bowl and serve.	Strain before pouring into a mug or bowl, then serve.

Supper

Chicken liver pâté

Classic chicken liver pâté is given an added depth of flavour by the addition of intense 100% chocolate. This makes a wonderful starter, or spread on crackers, or thin toast, and serve it as a canapé with drinks.

Ingredients

400g chicken livers

300g unsalted butter

1½ tbsp brandy

15g 100% dark chocolate flakes

Salt and black pepper

To serve

Delicious crackers, or thin toast.

Method

Pick over the chicken livers, and remove any yellowish bits with a sharp knife. Prepare your food processor by fitting the blade.

Heat 100g butter in a small heavy pan. Cook the livers in the butter for five minutes, turning constantly. The outsides should be browned but not toughened, and the insides pink but not raw. Remove the livers from the pan and place into the bowl of your food processor.

Pour brandy into the pan and allow it to sizzle for a moment. Sprinkle chocolate flakes onto the livers in the food processor, and add the remaining butter. Pour hot brandy from the pan over the livers, butter and chocolate.

Blend to a smooth paste, and season with salt and black pepper to taste. Use a spatula to transfer the mixture into a serving dish, smoothing down the surface. Cover with greaseproof paper, and chill in the fridge before serving.

K52

This is the Knoops take on a B52, a layered coffee liqueur shot. We have made our version with our own Crème de Knoops.

Serves

1

Ingredients

15ml Crème de Knoops
(p.128)

15ml Irish Cream

15ml Amaretto

Method

Layer ingredients in a shot glass, and serve.

Jealousy

We have two versions here, so make whichever takes your fancy. You can choose Crème de Menthe, or swap it for Chambord if you prefer raspberry.

Serves

4

Ingredients

100ml Crème de Knoops
(p.128)

50ml double cream

20ml Crème de Menthe or Chambord

Method

Divide Crème de Knoops between four shot glasses. Whisk cream with the Crème de Menthe (or Chambord). Then top each of the glasses with a spoon or two of the cream mixture and serve.

Chilli con carne

The rich, full flavours of this classic dish are deepened by the addition of 100% dark chocolate flakes. Serve with all your favourite sides for a warming, hearty supper.

Ingredients

1 tbsp olive oil

1 large yellow onion chopped

4 cloves garlic, thinly sliced

750g lean minced beef

250g pork fillets, diced into small chunks

125g cooking chorizo, cut into small chunks

1 tsp ground cumin

1 tsp cayenne pepper

Sea salt and ground pepper

2 red romano peppers

1 glass red wine

2 tbsp tomato puree

200ml passata

500ml beef stock

1 tin drained kidney beans or black beans

30g 100% dark chocolate flakes

To Serve

Plenty of roughly chopped coriander

Jasmine or long-grain rice

Tortilla chips

Lime wedges

Method

To make this dish, you will need a large casserole with a lid, suitable for use both on the hob and in the oven.

In the casserole, warm the oil and soften the chopped onion over a medium heat. Add the garlic.

Add beef, pork, and chorizo and brown on all sides over a medium heat, then season with the cumin, cayenne pepper, salt and ground pepper. Chop and deseed the peppers, and add to the casserole. Pour in the red wine and allow everything to bubble for a few minutes.

Add the tomato puree and passata, followed by the beef stock. Top up with enough water to just cover, and simmer over a low heat for about an hour with the lid on. Remove from the heat, stir, replace the lid, and leave the chilli to rest.

About an hour before you plan to serve, stir the beans into the chilli, replace the lid and cook in a preheated oven at 170°C (150°C fan), Gas 3, 325°F, for 60 minutes. Cook the rice according to the manufacturer's instructions, so it will be ready at the same time as the chilli.

Remove chilli from the oven and stir through the chocolate flakes to melt. Garnish with chopped coriander, and serve with cooked rice, tortilla chips and lime wedges.

Mulled wine with chocolate

Our special Knoops take on the most festive drink of all — warming, delicious and served in Christmas markets throughout Germany.

Ingredients

100ml red wine
(Pinot Noir is perfect)

100ml port

1 cinnamon stick

1 star anise

3 cloves

A thin slice of fresh ginger

400ml water

10½ tbsp (approx. 135g)
54% dark chocolate flakes

Method

Pour wine and port into a small pan and add the spices and ginger. Heat to a simmer, then remove from heat and leave to steep for an hour. Reheat to a simmer when you are ready to make your hot chocolate.

Heat the water to steaming point, then whisk in the chocolate or combine in a hot chocolate shaker. Strain the mulled wine and whisk into the hot chocolate. Divide between four mugs or glasses, and serve.

 Knoops Tip: For a creamier drink, use oat milk instead of water. Don't use dairy milk, as it will curdle.

Chocolate & raspberry soufflé cake

This rich and squidgy flourless cake is a delicious after-dinner treat. Sharp raspberries, with their soft, juicy texture and deep red colour, make the perfect complement to this dense and chocolatey cake. It is wonderful served at room temperature, when it will be firmer, but is at its best served slightly warm with cold raspberry ripple cream.

Ingredients

125g unsalted butter

200g 54% dark chocolate flakes

4 eggs, at room temperature

250g caster sugar

1 tsp vanilla paste

125g raspberries

To Serve

250g double cream or crème fraiche

100g icing sugar

175g raspberries

25g icing sugar

Handful of whole raspberries to decorate

Method

Preheat the oven to 170°C (150°C fan), Gas 3, 325°F. Line the base of a 20cm springform tin with baking paper.

Melt butter and chocolate together in a bowl over a pan of simmering water. Separate the eggs and whisk egg yolks with 150g of the caster sugar and the vanilla paste until pale and creamy. Fold the chocolate mixture and 125g raspberries carefully into the egg yolk mixture.

In a clean, dry bowl, beat the egg whites until they form soft peaks. Add the remaining 100g caster sugar, and continue whisking until combined. Loosen the chocolate mixture with one spoonful of the whisked egg whites. Add the rest of the whites and gently fold through until completely combined. Spread the batter evenly into the prepared tin.

Bake in the centre of the oven for 30 to 40 minutes, until the top starts to crack. The cake should still have a little wobble. A skewer should come out free of liquid mix but not completely clean, as this is a very tender, moist cake.

Remove the cake from the oven and place on a cooling rack. After 15 minutes, when cool enough to handle, remove the sides of the tin. It is easiest to serve this delicate cake from the base of the tin.

Whip the double cream to soft peaks with 100g icing sugar, or stir icing sugar into the crème fraiche if preferred. Mash 175g raspberries with 25g icing sugar and ripple the puree through the cream. Serve cake slices with the cream and extra raspberries.

Chocolate Irish coffee

A chocolate twist on the classic drink, created in 1943 by chef Joe Sheridan at Foynes airbase in Limerick. The original was glamorous at the time, and it's even better now we've updated it.

Ingredients

150ml hot coffee

2 tbsp Irish whiskey

8 tsp (approx. 34g) 54% dark chocolate flakes

1 tbsp unrefined caster sugar

4 tbsp softly whipped double cream

Method

Make coffee, using your preferred method. Add the chocolate flakes and sugar to the coffee to melt, and whisk until well combined. When smooth, add whiskey and mix, then divide between two glasses. Top each with half the whipped cream, sprinkle with a little extra chocolate, and serve.

Knoops Banshee

Bananas, chocolate and rum are a great combination.

Chocolate Brandy Alexander

The Brandy Alexander was supposedly John Lennon's favourite drink.

Knoops Jockey Club

This is our take on a traditional cocktail from the Jockey Club. The earliest versions on record date from the 1880s.

Serves

Serves

Serves

Ingredients

30ml rum

15ml banana liqueur

30ml Crème de Knoops (p.128)

60ml single cream

½ ripe banana

Ingredients

30ml Crème de Knoops (p.128)

30ml brandy

10ml double cream

Grating of nutmeg

Ice cubes

Ingredients

30ml gin

15ml hazelnut liqueur

15ml Crème de Knoops (p.128)

1½ tsp lemon juice

Dash of Angostura Bitters

Method

Blend all ingredients until smooth. Pour into a cocktail glass and serve.

Method

Put all ingredients except the nutmeg into a shaker, with a couple of ice cubes. Shake well, then strain into a cocktail glass. Top with grated nutmeg to serve.

Method

Shake or whisk all ingredients together Pour into a cocktail glass, add a thin slice of lemon rind, and serve.

Suzy's Knickerbocker Glory

This delicious retro pudding will delight the whole family. A combination of ice creams, fruit, berry coulis, marshmallows, honeycomb, sweets, biscuits and cream.... What's not to love?

Ingredients

200g strawberries

200g raspberries

4 large scoops vanilla ice cream

4 large Knoops marshmallows, cut into pieces

200g honeycomb pieces

Plums, peaches, apricots - or any fruit of your choice

4 large scoops chocolate or strawberry ice cream

White or ruby chocolate flakes, to sprinkle

Nuts, biscuit pieces, sweets of your choice

54% dark chocolate flakes

34% milk chocolate flakes

150ml whipping cream

4 macarons

4 glacé cherries

Method

First, make a coulis by mashing or blending half the berries to a pourable liquid.

Scoop the vanilla ice cream into four knickerbocker glory glasses and drizzle with the freshly-made coulis. Add marshmallow pieces, honeycomb, the remaining berries and other fruit (as desired) quartered or sliced into bite-sized pieces.

Add a scoop of chocolate or strawberry ice cream to each of the glasses. Sprinkle over white or ruby chocolate flakes, and layer more fruit, coulis, honeycomb, and nuts or sweets if using (small jelly sweets work well). Continue layering until each glass is full.

Melt a little of the dark or milk chocolate in a bowl over a saucepan of simmering water, and pour generously over each sundae.

Whip the cream, then swirl or pipe on top. Finish each glass with a macaron, or honeycomb pieces, and more melted ruby or dark chocolate. Sprinkle with the ruby, milk or dark chocolate flakes and, of course, add a cherry on top.

Have fun playing around with this one; excess is key to its success! Serve with long-handled spoons, and enjoy.

Spiced Christmas hot chocolate

We make something special in the stores to celebrate each Christmas. This one is inspired by the traditional speculoos recipe that originated during the 17th century in the Netherlands, and is made with the addition of some fresh orange zest.

Ingredients

200ml milk (or plant-based alternative)

3 tbsp (approximately 34 grams) of 54% dark chocolate flakes

1 tsp spice mix (see below)

½ tsp fresh grated orange zest from an unwaxed orange. If using a waxed orange, soak in hot water, scrub, and soak again in hot water to remove all wax before zesting.

Spice mix (makes 5 hot chocolates)

1 tbsp ground cinnamon

¾ tsp ground nutmeg

¾ tsp ground cloves

½ tsp ground ginger

½ tsp ground white pepper

¼ tsp ground cardamom

Method

Heat milk and add the chocolate flakes, and 1 tsp spice mix. Stir or whisk until fully dissolved. Add orange zest, and stir or whisk again.

Alternatively, place all ingredients into a chocolate shaker, and heat in the microwave for 1-2 minutes without the lid. Remove from the microwave, add the lid and shake for 10-15 seconds, until all ingredients are fully blended.

Pour into a hot chocolate mug, and serve immediately.

Chocolate dipping platter

After supper, what could be more fun than a platter of scrumptious fruits and sweets to scoop into a quartet of decadent chocolate dips?

Ingredients

200g 28% white chocolate flakes

200g 47% ruby chocolate flakes

200g 54% dark chocolate flakes

200g 100% dark chocolate flakes topped with 3-4 large Knoops marshmallows (or more if smaller).

To dip

Berries, especially blueberries, blackberries, raspberries, strawberries

Apples, pears, plums, peaches, grapes (or any other fruit you enjoy)

Pretzels, macarons, marshmallows

Honeycomb chunks

Popcorn

Method

First, make the dips. Take each of the first three types of chocolate flakes (white, ruby, and 54% dark) and melt them in small bowls over simmering water. Pour the melted chocolate into individual small dipping bowls.

Place the 100% dark chocolate flakes into a heatproof bowl and cover with 3-4 marshmallows, sliced. Place under the grill for 1-2 minutes, until marshmallows are melting and golden. Alternatively, heat in microwave for 20 seconds to melt.

Rinse and/or prepare all the dipping ingredients, cutting into bite-sized pieces if necessary. Arrange on a large board or serving platter, with enough wooden skewers for everyone. Add anything you like to our dipping suggestions; experiment to find your favourites.

Serve in the middle of the table for all to enjoy.

After Supper

S'mores

A bonfire night treat you can recreate any night of the year. Crunchy biscuits sandwich warm, melted chocolate and gooey, toasted marshmallow — pure happiness.

Ingredients

For the digestive biscuits

125g plain white flour

125g plain wholemeal flour

60g oatmeal

75g unrefined caster sugar

½ tsp bicarbonate of soda

¾ tsp salt

125g cold unsalted butter, cut into small cubes

4 tbsp milk

To make the s'mores

20 tsp (approx. 100g) 70% dark chocolate flakes

10 large Knoops marshmallows

Method

Put the flours, oatmeal, sugar, bicarbonate of soda and salt into a large bowl and mix them together. Then add the cold butter and rub it into the dry ingredients with your fingers until it is fully worked through and the mixture resembles rough breadcrumbs. Lastly add the milk and bring all together into a soft dough.

Wrap the dough in clingfilm and rest it in the fridge for 30 minutes. While the dough is chilling, preheat oven to 190°C (170°C fan), Gas 5, 375°F. Line two baking trays with baking paper.

Lightly flour a work surface and your rolling pin, and roll out the dough to a thickness of about 4mm. Using a rectangular cookie cutter, or a stencil 1cm larger than your marshmallows, cut the dough into biscuits, and place them on the prepared baking trays with a little space between each. You should get 20 biscuits out of the dough.

Bake biscuits for ten minutes, until they are golden at the edges. Remove from oven, and rest on trays for five minutes. Then transfer biscuits to a wire rack to cool completely. They will crisp up as they cool, and then you can make your s'mores!

Melt the chocolate flakes in a bowl over a saucepan of simmering water. Toast marshmallows one by one under the grill or on a fire pit, until charred and melting. Paint melted chocolate on one side of each biscuit. Place each toasted marshmallow on the chocolate side of a biscuit. Then sandwich with the second biscuit, chocolate side down. Eat while warm. Sensational.

Crème de Knoops

Dark, deliciously rich and decadent in its own right, this is also the basis of many more fabulous drinks. This recipe is dedicated to Cat Black; thank you for being such a passionate mentor.

Ingredients

200g 100% dark chocolate flakes

300ml vodka

250g unrefined caster sugar

500ml water

Method

Put the chocolate flakes and vodka into a saucepan over a gentle heat, warming just enough to melt the chocolate. Remove from the heat and blend with a hand whisk until the chocolate is dissolved and smoothly combined with the vodka.

In another pan, combine water and sugar and heat gently, stirring until the sugar is completely dissolved. Set aside to cool.

Once completely cooled, combine the sugar syrup with the chocolate and vodka. Mix well. Store at room temperature in a sealed bottle or jar with a well-fitted lid; this recipe makes approximately 1.2 litres.

Serve in small shot glasses, over ice, or use in other drinks (see our other recipes).

Biscotti

These twice-baked favourites combine crunchy biscuit and toasted hazelnuts with chocolate for a sensational after-dinner treat. They also make great gifts!

Ingredients

200g very roughly chopped hazelnuts, (plus a handful finely chopped for decorating)

3 eggs

230g unrefined caster sugar

½ tsp vanilla extract

Pinch of salt

Zest of one lemon

430g plain flour (you may need a little extra for dusting).

1 tsp baking powder

For dipping

100g 70% dark chocolate flakes

Method

Preheat oven to 180°C (160°C fan), Gas 4, 350°F.
Line a baking sheet with baking paper.

Toast the hazelnuts in a dry frying pan until they start to colour and release a delicious aroma. Set them aside to cool.

Separate the eggs. Mix yolks, sugar and vanilla in a large bowl to form a paste. Whisk egg whites and salt until firm. Loosen the yolks mixture by stirring in a spoonful of the whites, and then lightly fold through the rest. Mix chopped hazelnuts with lemon zest, and then gently fold into the mixture as well. Finally, sieve the flour and baking powder together and add. Fold to combine.

Work the dough by hand for a minute or so, then shape into two long fat rolls. It will be sticky, so handle carefully with floured hands. Resist adding more flour to the dough. Place the rolls onto the prepared baking sheet, side by side. Flatten each a little, so they look like long flat loaves. Bake for 30 minutes, until lightly golden.

Remove from the oven, and immediately cut each loaf into thin (1-cm) slices. Use an oven glove to hold the hot loaf while you slice with a serrated knife. Lay the individual biscotti out on the baking sheet and return them to the oven. Bake for no more than five minutes, then turn them over and bake for five more minutes on the other side. Cool on a wire rack.

Melt chocolate in a small bowl over simmering water. Dip the end of each biscotti into the chocolate, then sprinkle with chopped hazelnuts. Rest on greaseproof paper to allow the chocolate to set. Store in an airtight container.

Calming, comforting and, most importantly, delicious, these late-evening drinks will help you wind down, tune out and ease into a peaceful night's sleep.

Knoovaltine

This is our version of the bedtime classic. This makes a whole jar, so you can stir up a warming mugful easily, no matter how tired you feel.

Serves

20

Ingredients

200g malt powder

200g milk powder

400g 34% milk chocolate flakes

Method

Combine ingredients and store in an airtight jar in a cool, dry place. To make one cup of Knoovaltine, place five heaped teaspoons of your mixture in a mug. Fill the mug with boiling water. Stir well to melt and mix before drinking. This recipe makes enough for approximately 20 servings.

Hot chocolate with chamomile & valerian

Chamomile and valerian are traditionally used for their soothing and soporific qualities. This is my grandmother's recipe for a bedtime drink that would help her sleep soundly.

Serves

1

Ingredients

200ml whole milk

1 tsp dried valerian root

1 tsp chamomile flowers

1 tsp honey (floral honey works especially well)

8 tsp (approx. 34g) 54% chocolate flakes

Method

Heat milk with valerian and chamomile. When the milk is steaming, strain and pour over the honey and chocolate flakes, whisking to combine and melt the chocolate (or combine in a chocolate shaker).

Pour and serve.

A final treat last thing at night; these luxurious drinks are to be sipped and lingered over at the end of a long day, paving the way to sweet dreams.

Death by chocolate

This is a wonderfully grown-up version of a chocolate milkshake. Rich, indulgent and full-on chocolatey.

Serves

Ingredients

60g chocolate ice cream

20ml Irish cream liqueur

20ml Crème de Knoops (see p. 128)

20ml vodka

Method

Place all the ingredients in a blender, or use a stick blender and a jug. Blend until smooth.

Pour into a glass and serve immediately.

Night cap

The classic sleep remedy is a milky drink. The flavours of a comforting rice pudding and a tot of rum make this version especially warming.

Serves

Ingredients

200ml whole milk

8 tsp (approx. 34g) 28% white chocolate flakes

Freshly grated nutmeg (and extra to top)

2 tbsp rum or cognac (as preferred)

Method

Heat milk and whisk with chocolate and a generous grating of nutmeg to combine and allow the chocolate to melt. If using a hot chocolate mixer, combine the milk, chocolate and nutmeg and heat together..

Pour rum into a mug, then pour over the hot chocolate blend. Top with grated nutmeg before serving.

Conversion tables

°C	Fan	Gas	°F
140	120	1	275
150	130	2	300
160/170	140/150	3	325
180	160	4	350
190	170	5	375
200	180	6	400
220	200	7	425
230	210	8	450
240	220	9	475

Spoons	Metric
¼ teaspoon	1ml
½ teaspoon	2.5ml
¾ teaspoon	4ml
1 teaspoon	5ml
1 dessertspoon	10ml
1 tablespoon	15ml

Metric	Imperial	Cups
15ml	½ fl oz	1 tablespoon
30ml	1 fl oz	⅛ cup
60ml	2 fl oz	¼ cup
75ml	2½ fl oz	⅓ cup
120ml	4 fl oz	½ cup
150ml	5 fl oz	⅔ cup
180ml	6 fl oz	¾ cup
250ml	8 fl oz	1 cup

Imperial	Metric
½oz	15g
¾oz	20g
1oz	30g
2oz	60g
3oz	85g
4oz	115g
5oz	140g
6oz	170g
7oz	200g
8oz	230g
9oz	255g
10oz	285g
11oz	310g
12oz	340g
13 z	370g
14oz	400g
15oz	425g
16oz	450g
24 z	680g
32oz	900g

Stockists

All the Knoops chocolate flakes, coffee, marshmallows and equipment mentioned in this book are available on-line from knoops.co.uk and from the shops listed here. Where possible, use the chocolate percentage specified, as each recipe has been created around that exact flavour and strength.

Knoops chocolate flakes
All the flakes below are sold in tubes, and all of 54% and above are vegan.
* 28% White Chocolate Flakes
* 34% Milk Chocolate Flakes
* 43% Milk Chocolate Flakes - Single Origin - Venezuela
* 47% Ruby Chocolate Flakes
* 54% Dark Chocolate Flakes
* 65% Dark Chocolate Flakes Single Origin - Colombia
* 70% Extra Dark Chocolate Flakes
* 72% Extra Dark Chocolate Flakes Single Origin - Peru
* 80% Extra Dark Chocolate Flakes
* 100% Extra Dark Chocolate Flakes Single Origin - Solomon Islands

Knoops marshmallows
Marshmallows are available individually instore, and in 130g tubes.

Knoops coffee
Coffee is available in 250g packs.
* Knoops Speciality Ground Coffee Honduras: Aldea Capucas – 100% Arabica
* Knoops Speciality Coffee Beans Honduras: Aldea Capucas – 100% Arabica

Equipment
* Chocolate Shaker
* Hot Chocolate Drinking Bowls
* A wide selection of chocolate drink and coffee makers

Knoops stores

* **Rye** - Tower Forge, Hilders Cliff, Rye, East Sussex, TN31 7LD

* **Clapham Junction** - 64 St. John's Road, London, SW11 1PS

* **Kensington** - 80 Kensington High Street, London, W8 4SG

* **Chelsea** - 69 King's Road, London, SW3 4NT

* **Brighton** - 42 Market Street, Brighton, BN1 1HH

* **Richmond** - 1 George Street, Richmond, TW9 1JY

Thanks

All my thanks go to the following people for all their hard work, inspiration and forbearance; without them this book would never have been possible.
Suzy Clode, Cat Black, Mark Calderbank at Reason Design, Jamie Lau at Studio Lau Photography, Tory Gordon-Harris, Lola Faure, Penelope Parker, Susan Kelly, Martin Koffer at Gomer Press Ltd. William Gordon-Harris and everyone at Knoops Holdings Ltd.

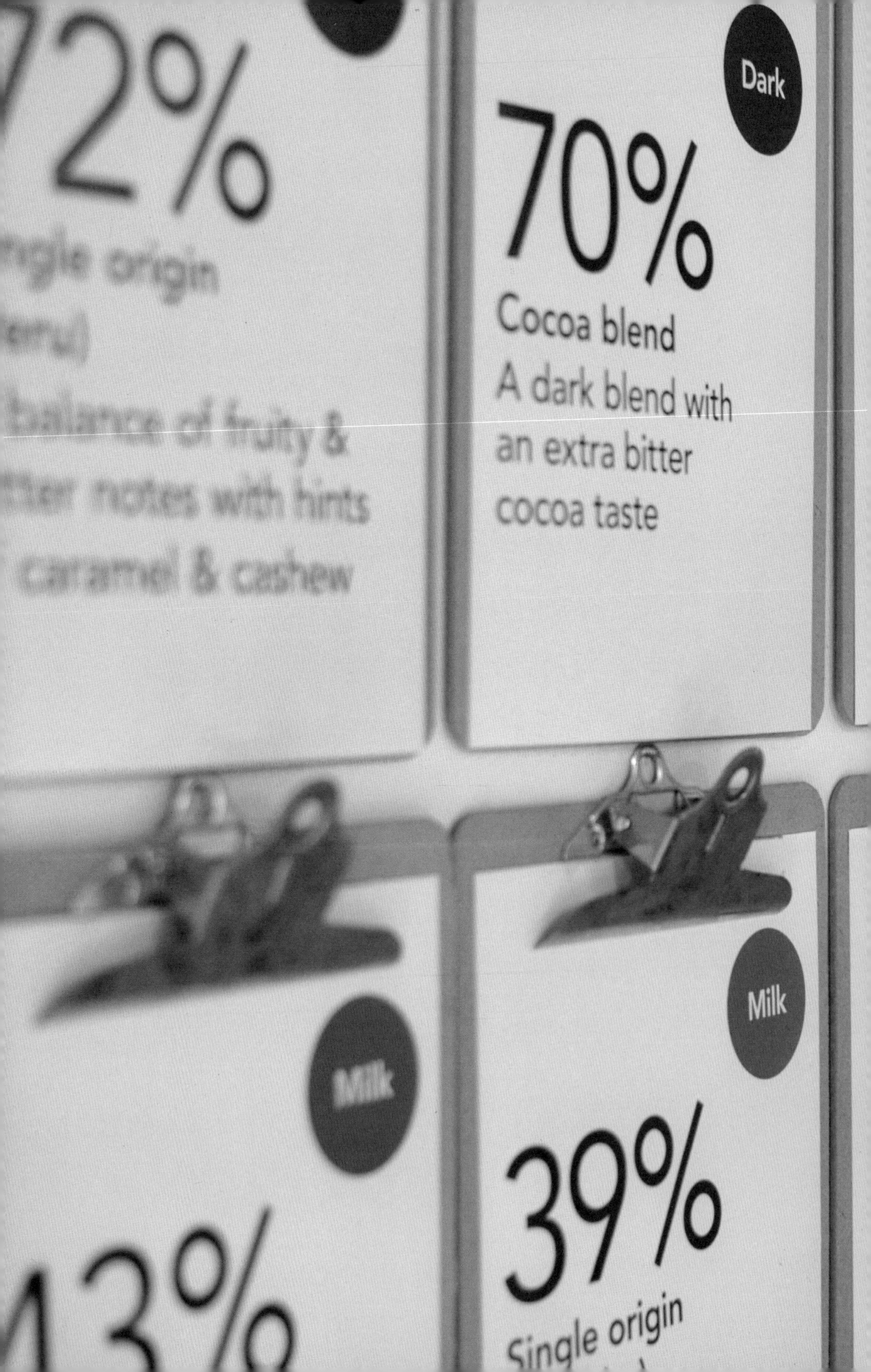

72%

ngle origin
(Peru)

balance of fruity &
tter notes with hints
caramel & cashew

70%

Cocoa blend
A dark blend with
an extra bitter
cocoa taste

Milk

Milk

43%

39%

Single origin